Assertiveness and Self-Control

90 Minute Guides

Michelle N. Halsey

Silver City Publications & Training, L.L.C.
P.O. Box 1914
Nampa, ID 83653
https://www.silvercitypublications.com/shop/

ISBN-10: 1640040056
ISBN-13: 978-1-64004-005-2

Contents

Chapter 1 – What Does Self Confidence Mean to You?

Self-confidence plays an important role in our everyday lives. Being confident allows us to set and reach our goals. It provides stability when we are faced with a challenge; it gives us that push that helps us overcome difficulties. Self-confidence is necessary in our personal and professional lives, as without it one would not be successful in either. It gives us the ability to stand up to face our challenges and to pick ourselves up when we fall.

What is Assertiveness?

An assertive person is confident and direct in dealing with others. Assertive communications promote fairness and equality in human interactions, based on a positive sense of respect for self and others. It is the direct communication of a person's needs, wants, and opinions without punishing, threatening, or putting down another person.

Assertive behavior includes the ability to stand up for a person's legitimate rights – without violating the rights of others or being overly fearful in the process. A skill that can be learned, assertive behavior is situational specific; meaning different types of assertive behavior can be used in different situations.

Assertive behavior involves three categories of skills; self-affirmation, expressing positive feelings, and expressing negative feelings. Each will be explored during this course.

What is Self-Confidence?

Self-confidence is a belief in oneself, one's abilities, or one's judgment. It is freedom from doubt. When you believe you can change things -- or make a difference in a situation, you are much more likely to succeed.

As a self-confident person, you walk with a bounce in your step. You can control your thoughts and emotions and influence others. You are more prepared to tackle everyday challenges and recover from setbacks. This all leads to a greater degree of optimism and life satisfaction.

Chapter 2 – The Four Styles

There are four styles of communication: passive, aggressive, passive-aggressive, and assertive.

The Passive Person

Passive behavior is the avoidance of the expression of opinions or feelings, protecting one's rights, and identifying and meeting one's needs. Passive individuals exhibit poor eye contact and slumped body posture, and tend to speak softly or apologetically. Passive people express statements implying that:

- "I'm unable to stand up for my rights."

- "I don't know what my rights are."

- "I get stepped on by everyone."

- "I'm weak and unable to take care of myself."

- "People never consider my feelings."

The Aggressive Person

An aggressive individual communicates in a way that violates the rights of others. Thus, aggressive communicators are verbally or physically abusive, or both. Aggressive communication is born of low self-esteem, often caused by past physical or emotional abuse, unhealed emotional wounds, and feelings of powerlessness.

Aggressive individuals display a low tolerance for frustration, use humiliation, interrupt frequently, and use criticism or blame to attack others. They use piercing eye contact, and are not good listeners. Aggressive people express statements implying that:

- The other person is inferior, wrong, and not worth anything

- The problem is the other person's fault

- They are superior and right

- They will get their way regardless of the consequences

- They are entitled, and that the other person "owes" them.

The Passive-Aggressive Person

The passive-aggressive person uses a communication style in which the individual appears passive on the surface, but is really acting out anger in a subtle, indirect, or behind-the-scenes way.

Passive-aggressive people usually feel powerless, stuck, and resentful. Alienated from others, they feel incapable of dealing directly with the object of their resentments. Rather, they express their anger by subtly undermining the real or imagined object of their resentments. Frequently they mutter to themselves instead of confronting another person. They often smile at you, even though they are angry, use subtle sabotage, or speak with sarcasm.

Passive-aggressive individuals use communication that implies:

- "I'm weak and resentful, so I sabotage, frustrate, and disrupt."

- "I'm powerless to deal with you head on so I must use guerilla warfare."

- "I will appear cooperative, but I'm not."

The Assertive Person

An assertive individual communicates in a way that clearly states his or her opinions and feelings, and firmly advocates for his or her rights and needs without violating the rights of others. Assertive communication is born of high self-esteem. Assertive people value themselves, their time, and their emotional, spiritual, and physical needs. They are strong advocates for themselves -- while being very respectful of the rights of others.

Assertive people feel connected to other people. They make statements of needs and feelings clearly, appropriately, and respectfully. Feeling in control of themselves, they speak in calm and clear tones, are good listeners, and maintain good eye contact. They create a respectful environment for others, and do not allow others to abuse or manipulate them.

The assertive person uses statements that imply:

- "I am confident about who I am."

- "I cannot control others, but I control myself."

- "I speak clearly, honestly, and to the point."

- "I know I have choices in my life, and I consider my options. I am fully responsible for my own happiness."

- "We are equally entitled to express ourselves respectfully to one another."

Chapter 3 – Obstacles to Our Goals

Obstacles are encountered every day of our lives, but what we do and how we react during these events will determine the outcomes of such events. Our reactions to these obstacles will determine if the situation becomes a minor annoyance to a major event. Over reacting to a small annoyance can magnify the issue and make larger than it actually is. These are the types of reactions that should be kept in check, what is an appropriate response to each obstacle that we encounter? Like many things the obstacle will determine the response.

Types of Negative Thinking

Negative thinking is the process of thinking negative rather than positive thoughts. Seemingly, positive thinking requires effort while negative thinking is uninvited and happens easily.

A person who has been brought up in a happy and positive atmosphere, where people value success and self-improvement will have a much easier time thinking positively. One who was brought up in a poor or difficult situation will probably continue to expect difficulties and failure.

Negative thoughts center on the individual, others, and the future. Negative thinking causes problems such as depression, pessimism, and anxiety. Typical types of negative thinking are described below.

Type of Thinking	As the thinker, you:
Overgeneralization	Make a general universal rule from one isolated event
Global labeling	Automatically use disparaging labels to describe yourself
Filtering	Pay attention selectively to the negative, disregarding the positive
Polarized thinking	Group things into absolute, black and white categories, assuming that you must be perfect or you are worthless
Self-blame	Persistently blame yourself for things that may not be your fault
Personalization	Assume that everything has something to do with you, negatively comparing yourself to

	everyone else
Mind reading	Feel that people don't like you or are angry with you, without any real evidence
Control fallacies	Feel that you have total responsibility for everybody and everything, or that you have no control as a helpless victim
Emotional reasoning	Believe that things are the way you feel about them

Personal Application

We all have situations in our personal lives where the ability to be assertive helps us achieve our goals. Now we'll each practice the opportunity to develop assertive responses. Standing up for yourself will translate into success throughout your personal and professional lives. It will help grow a person's self-confidence, and make the challenges that we encounter every day that much more easily to overcome.

Chapter 4 – Communication Skills

Strong communication skills are essential for assertive interaction with others. Humans are social animals and communication is a very important part of our daily lives. Every interaction we have with another person including, face to face, over the phone, chatting online or even texting is communication happening, and have strong communication skills will benefit every type of interaction we encounter.

Listening and Hearing; They Aren't the Same Thing

Hearing is the act of perceiving sound by the ear. Assuming an individual is not hearing-impaired, hearing simply happens. Listening, however, is something that one consciously chooses to do. Listening requires concentration so that the brain processes meaning from words and sentences.

Listening leads to learning, but this is not always an easy task. The normal adult rate of speech is 100-150 words per minute, but the brain can think at a rate of 400-500 words per minute, leaving extra time for daydreaming, or anticipating the speaker's or the recipient's next words.

As opposed to hearing, listening skills can be learned and refined. The art of active listening allows you to fully receive a message from another person. Especially in a situation involving anger or a tense interchange, active listening allows you to be sensitive to the multiple dimensions of communication that make up an entire message. These dimensions include:

The occasion for the message: What is the reason why the person is communicating with me now?

The length of the message: What can the length of the message tell me about its importance?

The words chosen: Is the message being made formally? Is it with aloofness or slang?

The volume and pace: What clues do the loudness and speed give me?

The Pauses and Hesitations: How do these enhance or detract from the message?

Non-verbal clues: What does eye contact, posture, or facial expressions tell me about the message?

Empathy is the capability to share and understand another's emotions and feelings. Empathetic listening is the art of seeking a truer understanding of how others are feeling. This requires excellent discrimination and close attention to the nuances of emotional signals. According to Stephen Covey in "The Seven Habits of Highly Effective People", empathetic listening involves five basic tasks:

1. Repeat verbatim the content of the communication; the words, not the feelings

2. Rephrase content; summarize the meaning of the words in your own words

3. Reflect feelings; look more deeply and begin to capture feelings in your own words. Look beyond words for body language and tone to indicate feelings.

4. Rephrase contents and reflect feelings; express both their words and feelings in your own words.

5. Discern when empathy is not necessary – or appropriate.

Asking Questions

Active listeners use specific questioning techniques to elicit more information from speakers. Below are three types of questions to use when practicing active listening.

Open Questions

Open questions stimulate thinking and discussion or responses including opinions or feelings. They pass control of the conversation to the respondent. Leading words in open questions include: *Why, what, or how*, as in the following examples:

- Tell me about the current employee orientation process.

- How do you open the emergency exit door on an A320 aircraft?

Clarifying Questions

A clarifying question helps to remove ambiguity, elicits additional detail, and guides the answer to a question. When you ask a clarifying question, you ask for expansion or detail, while withholding your judgment and own opinions. When asking for clarification, you will have to listen carefully to what the other person says. Frame your question as someone trying to understand in more detail. Often asking for a specific example is useful. This also helps the speaker evaluate his or her own opinions and perspective. Below are some examples:

- I can tell you are really concerned about this. Let me see if I can repeat to you your main concerns so we can start to think about what to do in this situation.

- What sort of savings are you looking to achieve?

Closed Questions

Closed questions usually require a one-word answer, and effectively shut off discussion. Closed questions provide facts, allow the questioner to maintain control of the conversation, and are easy to answer. Typical leading words are: *Is, can, how many, or does*. While closed questions are not the optimum choice for active listening, at times they may be necessary to elicit facts. Below are several examples of closed questions:

- Who will lead the meeting?

- Do you know how to open the emergency exit door on this aircraft?

The following exercise provides practice with questioning techniques to support communications skills.

Chapter 5 – Body Language

Body language is a form of non-verbal communication involving the use of stylized gestures, postures, and physiologic signs which act as cues to other people. Humans unconsciously send and receive non-verbal signals through body language all the time.

Non-verbal communication is the process of communication through sending and receiving wordless messages. It is the single most powerful form of communication. Nonverbal communication cues others about what is in your mind, even more than your voice or words can do.

According to studies at UCLA, as much as 93 percent of communication effectiveness is determined by nonverbal cues, and the impact of performance was determined 7 percent by the words used, 38 percent by voice quality, and 55 percent by non-verbal communication.

In communication, if a conflict arises between your words and your body language, your body language rules every time.

The Role of Body Language

Body language is a form of non-verbal communication involving the use of stylized gestures, postures, and physiologic signs which act as cues to other people. Humans unconsciously send and receive non-verbal signals through body language all the time.

One study at UCLA found that up to 93 percent of communication effectiveness is determined by nonverbal cues. Another study indicated that the impact of a performance was determined 7 percent by the words used, 38 percent by voice quality, and 55 percent by non-verbal communication. Your body language must match the words used. If a conflict arises between your words and your body language, your body language governs. The components of body language include:

Eye contact: The impact of your message is affected by the amount of eye contact you maintain with the person with whom you are speaking. One who makes eye contact is normally perceived as more favorable and confident.

Posture: Find comfortable sitting and standing postures that work for you; avoid any rigid or slouching positions.

Excessive or unrelated head, facial, hand and body Movement: Too much movement can divert attention from the verbal message. Your facial expressions should match the type of statement you are making; smile when saying "I like you", and frowning when saying "I am annoyed with you". Occasional gestures that reinforce your verbal message are acceptable.

First Impressions Count

It takes as few as seven seconds – and no more than thirty seconds -- for someone to form a first impression about you. Like it or not, people make judgments about others right away based on a presenting appearance. And you never have a second chance to make a first impression. Below are some tips to help you make that positive first impression when someone.

- **Body language.** Remember that body language makes up to 55% of a communication.

- **Dress and grooming.** It's less about your budget, and more about clean, pressed, and event-appropriate clothing with neat grooming.

- **Handshake.** Use a medium to firm handshake grip, avoiding a weak handshake, or overly firm one that can cause potential discomfort to another.

- **Body Movement.** Use a mirror, or enlist the help of a friend to make sure that your movements are not overly active --and that they support the nature of your message.

Chapter 6 – The Importance of Goal Setting

A strong self-concept depends both upon what you do, and your idea of yourself. Goal setting is the process that allows you to analyze and determine what you do. Goal setting helps you feel strong and in control. Goal setting drives us and gives us a measure for our successes. Setting goals provides an incentive and helps to push us into completing the goals we set.

Why Goal Setting is Important

The process of setting goals helps to provide a clear picture of your wants and needs so you can chart your own life destiny. To get a clear picture of your wants and needs, consider eight types of goals.

To begin building and qualifying your list of goals, answer four key questions that serve as triggers.

Question	Example	Potential Goal
What hurts, or feels bad?	The long commute to work	Explore a telecommuting option
What are you hungry for?	More time in the outdoors	Plan a national park vacation
What are your dreams?	Enhance the yard	Build a rock garden
What are the little comforts?	A new kitten	Adopt or buy a pet

Now classify the goals according to potential timing: long-range, medium-range, and immediate.

Long-Range Goals

Explore a telecommuting option

Medium-Range Goals

Plan a national park vacation

Immediate

Get a kitten

Setting SMART Goals

The SMART method is a straightforward way to qualify and quantify each goal.

Handout Four: Smart Goal Setting describes the SMART criteria and provides examples of how they are used to establish and qualify goals.

SMART is a convenient acronym for the set of criteria that a goal must have in order for it to be realized by the goal achiever.

- **Specific**: Success coach Jack Canfield states in his book The Success Principles that, "Vague goals produce vague results." In order for you to achieve a goal, you must be very clear about what exactly you want. Often creating a list of benefits that the accomplishment of your goal will bring to your life, will you give your mind a compelling reason to pursue that goal.

- **Measurable**: It's crucial for goal achievement that you are able to track your progress towards your goal. That's why all goals need some form of objective measuring system so that you can stay on track and become motivated when you enjoy the sweet taste of quantifiable progress.

- **Achievable**: Setting big goals is great, but setting unrealistic goals will just de-motivate you. A good goal is one that challenges, but is not so unrealistic that you have virtually no chance of accomplishing it.

- **Relevant**: Before you even set goals, it's a good idea to sit down and define your core values and your life purpose because it's these tools which ultimately decide how and what goals you choose for your life. Goals, in and of themselves, do not provide any happiness. Goals that are in harmony with our life purpose do have the power to make us happy.

- **Timed**: Without setting deadlines for your goals, you have no real compelling reason or motivation to start working on them. By setting a deadline, your subconscious mind begins to work on that goal, night and day, to bring you closer to achievement.

Our Challenge to You

Use the SMART goal-setting method to set up an out of class personal goal.

- **Specific**: Be clear on what the goal will be.

- **Measurable**: Make it so you can track your progress.

- **Achievable**: Set a reasonable and achievable goal.

- **Relevant**: Make it relevant to your life at that moment.

- **Timed**: Set a deadline.

Chapter 7 – Feeling the Part

Being positive and feeling good about one's self is the key, you must feel the part. Positivity is a leading factor in one's self confidence, it will help you keep a feeling of worth. Staying positive will provide you a great asset in regards to self-talk and recognizing and working with your strengths. Everyone has weaknesses and by being positive you can recognize your weaknesses and then work on them to lesson to remove them all together.

Identifying Your Worth

Worth is defined as "sufficiently good, important, or interesting to justify a specified action." People with a sense of self-worth exude confidence in themselves. They feel in change of their own destiny, and are happy. To create a picture of your self-worth, take a self-concept inventory, analyzing multiple attributes in your life.

Attribute	Description
Physical appearance	Height, weight, facial appearance, skin, hair, style of dress, body areas
How you relate to others	Co-workers, friends, family, and strangers in social settings
Personality	Positive and negative personality traits
How other people see you	Positive and negative perceptions, as viewed by others
Performance at work or school	How you handle major tasks
Performance of the daily tasks of life	How you handle health, hygiene, maintenance of your living environment, food preparation, caring for children or parents
Mental functioning	How you reason and solve problems, your capacity for learning and creativity, your knowledge, wisdom, insights

Creating Positive Self-Talk

Positive self-talk allows you to recognize, validate, and apply your full potential with respect to all that you are, and do. Also called affirmations (to make something firm), positive self-talk serves as your own personal accomplishment scale. Below are some tips for positive self-talk:

- Use the present tense; deal with what exists today.

- Be positive – rather than affirming what you don't want.

- Remain personal; self-talk must relate to you and you only.

- Keep sentences short and simple.

- Go with your gut. If it "clicks", then just say it. Self-talk should feel positive, expanding, freeing, and supporting.

- Focus on new things, rather than changing what is.

- Act "as if"; give yourself permission to believe the idea is true right now.

If self-talk is new to you, it is a good idea to first think about the things that are wonderful about you, such as:

- I have someone I love, and we enjoy spending time together

- I am a mother or father, fulfilled in this role

- My career is challenging and fulfilling.

- When I learn something new, I feel proud.

- I am worthwhile because I breathe and feel; I am aware.

- When I feel pain, I love, I try to survive. I am a good person.

Identifying and Addressing Strengths and Weaknesses

After an individual has listed words and phrases for self-attributes, they can be classified as strengths or weaknesses. This exercise also allows participants to re-frame weaknesses into message that don't feed a negative self-worth.

Looking the Part

A person who has a strong sense of personal worth makes a confident, positive appearance. Looking the part is important as it influences the people around us. It will provide a boost to confidence and in turn a boost to your performance. Once higher performance is obtained it will then cycle back and make us more confident. Looking the part is an important part of being more assertive and confident as it is relatively quick and easy to do and pays off great dividends.

The Importance of Appearance

In the dictionary, appearance is defined as an external show, or outward aspect. Your confidence depends significantly on your personal thoughts and perceptions about the way you look. Appearance is as important today as it ever was. The first thing noticed when meeting someone new is their appearance. That is why it is important as you only have one first impression.

Chapter 8 – Sounding the Part

Feeling and looking the part would not be complete without voice. Given that we know that 38% of communication effectiveness is governed by voice quality, improving your overall voice message delivery is worthwhile.

It's How You Say It

We are all born with a particular tone of voice, which we can learn to improve. The goal is to sound upbeat, warm, under control, and clear. Here are some tips to help you begin the process.

1. Breathe from your diaphragm

2. Drink plenty of water to stay hydrated; avoid caffeine because of its diuretic effects

3. Posture affects breathing, and also tone of voice, so be sure to stand up straight

4. To warm up the tone of your voice, smile

5. If you have a voice that is particularly high or low, exercise it's by practicing speaking on a sliding scale. You can also sing to expand the range of your voice.

6. Record your voice and listen to the playback

7. Deeper voices are more credible than higher pitched voices. Try speaking in a slightly lower octave. It will take some practice, but with a payoff, just as radio personalities have learned

8. Enlist a colleague or family member to get feedback about the tone of your voice.

Sounding Confident

Since 38% of the messages received by a listener are governed by the tone and quality of your voice, its pitch, volume and control all make a difference in how confident you sound when you communicate. Below are some specific tips.

Pitch (Pitch means how high or low your voice is.) Tip: Avoid a high-pitched sound. Speak from your stomach, the location of your diaphragm.

Volume (The loudness of your voice must be governed by your diaphragm.) Tip: Speak through your diaphragm, not your throat

Quality (The color, warmth, and meaning given to your voice contribute to quality.) Tip: Add emotion to your voice. Smile as much as possible when you are speaking.

The need for assertive, confident communication can occur at any time, in virtually any place. So how do you make this all come together? Here are some practice suggestions.

- Start simply and gain some experience in safe environments, such as at the grocery store, or with family or friends

- Set aside time when you can read out loud without being disturbed; listen to yourself

- Challenge yourself to speak with someone new every day

- Set a realistic time frame to make the shift; don't expect to change your speaking style overnight.

Reducing Anxiety

Often, anxiety inhibits your ability to act and sound confident when speaking. Knowing how to perform a quick relaxation exercise can help diffuse anxiety and allow you to speak more confidently.

Using "I" Messages

An "I" message is a statement specifically worded to express your feelings about a particular situation. "I" messages begin with "I", and are an excellent way to share your feelings about particular behaviors -- without accusing the other person. There are four types of "I" messages, each with varying parts.

Chapter 9 – Powerful Presentations

Presentations made by assertive, self-confident people can achieve the desired outcome. What can be more confident building than giving a powerful presentation? Being prepared is the main tool in giving a powerful presentation. Preparedness provides you with the ability to be ready when the unexpected happens, or when you are called upon to speak up or give a presentation.

What to Do When You're on the Spot

Regardless of the situation, things are guaranteed to happen, and not always according to plan. Irrespective of the presentation venue, four actions can help you convert an interruption into an opportunity.

1. Always expect the unexpected!

2. At the beginning of the program, "work" the audience to pre-frame them, to create a mindset. Through light remarks, humor, or other responses based on your read of the group, leads them to make commitments to be playful, curious, flexible, and energized.

3. Create several positive anchors that you can use later. An anchor is something unique that you do or say that automatically puts the audience in a resourceful or emotional state. Examples include: A unique smile, specific place where you stand, the word "yes" in a strong voice.

4. If something unexpected happens, first smile, and then quickly ask yourself "How can I turn this event into an opportunity to create humor or illustrate a point?"

Using STAR to Make Your Case

STAR is an acronym that stands for **Situation or Task, Thoughts and Feelings, Actions, Results**. The STAR Model helps you deal with recurring problem situations such as repeated mental blocks or anxieties stemming from interpersonal situations. Using the four points of a star as the visual representation, the STAR model prompts questions that allow you to analyze the aspects of a problem situation -- and turn it around.

Coping Techniques

An assertive, self-confident person uses a variety of coping techniques to deal with the challenges of interpersonal communication. Many of these techniques come from the school of neuro-linguistic programming. NLP began in California in the mid-1970s, when graduate Richard Bandler joined a group at the University of Santa Cruz headed by linguistics professor John Grinder. NLP is defined as models and techniques to help understand and improve communication -- and to enhance influencing behavior.

Building Rapport

Rapport is the relation of harmony, conformity, accord, or affinity to support an outcome. The intended outcome is more likely with rapport than if it is not present. There is a sense of a shared understanding with another person.

Mirroring – matching certain behaviors of a person with whom you are interacting -- is the process used to establish rapport. There are four techniques for mirroring to build rapport.

- Voice tone or tempo

- Matching breathing rate

- Matching movement rhythms

- Matching body postures

Levels of rapport range on a continuum from a low of tolerance to a high of seduction. For business, strive for levels of neutral, lukewarm, understanding, identification, or warm, all in the center of the continuum.

Expressing Disagreement

Representations systems determine by the brain give us cues about how individuals process information. People can be classified as predominantly:

- **Visual** (The things we see)

- **Auditory** (The things we hear)

- **Kinesthetic** (The things we feel, touch, taste, or smell)

Both the type of words used, and the speaker's eye movement provide indicators of the system type. In a conversation, once we understand which type our conversation partner is, we can use the same system language to match the person's type, helping to ensure more reception to our message.

Coming to Consensus

Whether there is a disagreement on a particular issue, or you simply need to get a group to agree, neuro-linguistics offers a solution. To plan, make the following decisions:

1. What do you want your outcome to be?

2. How will you know when the outcome is achieved?

3. Who will attend the meeting? (Important: Each person invited to the meeting must have information needed for two out of three agenda items.)

Then, establish rapport as participants come into the meeting.

Now you are ready to use the **PEGASUS** model to achieve your desired outcomes.

Present outcomes
Explain evidence
Gain agreement on outcomes
Activate sensory acuity
Summarize each major decision
Use the relevancy challenge
Summarize the next step.

Dealing with Difficult Behavior

Each of us can probably think of at least one difficult personality with whom we have had to deal with, either at work or in our personal lives. With a strategy, it is possible to learn what the person does to annoy you, and what you might be doing to aggravate the situation.

Dealing with Difficult Situations

A difficult person can be your boss, your co-worker, or anyone else. He or she behaves in a way that is disruptive to business or life outside of work. In a work setting, often the functioning of a team is disturbed leading to a disruption of the work flow, flared tempers, and gossip. The bottom line is that work suffers and difficult situations cost organizations money.

To deal with difficult people, we innately try to apply coping filters, such as:

- Removing virtually all positive attributes about the person. ("He was my worst hiring mistake…")

- Defaming him or her (We build consensus with others against the person)

- Explaining the person in negative terms.

Anger also plays a big part; feeling angry, we instinctively use anger to try to manage the situation.

To break the cycle of negativity, take time to answer the following questions:

- What observable behaviors or statements did the person perform or say?

- What is the most positive interpretation an outside witness would make? The most negative?

- What will you gain by interpreting the difficult person's actions or words in as positive a light as possible?

- What would you do or say when you respond to the difficult person if you viewed his or her actions in a positive light? What is stopping you from responding this way?

Chapter 10 – Key Tactics

Three strategies will help you gather facts and use targeted strategies to deal with the person or the situation.

Active Listening

The first tactic, and possibly the most important, is to listen empathetically, which is listening while trying to be sensitive to the various components and levels of the message. We've already learned some strategies in module four for active listening. In addition, try to listen for the following information:

- **The Why:** Why is the person communicating with me?

- **The Length:** What can the size of the message tell me about the importance of the message to the person?

- **The Words:** Does the person use formal, aloof language? Impatience?

- The **Volume and Pace**: What emotional pressures can be sensed?

Note taking after a Discussion

A second tactic is to write down your recollection of the discussion that just took place. The notes can be used to support your next communication with the difficult person. Note taking also gives you the opportunity to plan and organize before the next communication takes place.

Writing Your Communication

Putting your thoughts into writing has three important benefits:

- The difficult person cannot interrupt with an objection

- It's easier to provide orderly communication in writing than in a discussion

- Written communication is pure; there is no body language to shape the outcome, reducing the possibility of mixed messages.

Additional Titles

The 90 Minute Guide series of books covers a variety of general business skills and are intended to be completed in 90 minutes or less. It is an effective way for building your skill set and can be used to acquire professional development units needed by project managers and other industries to maintain their certification. For the availability of titles please see

https://www.silvercitypublications.com/shop/.

No. 1 - Appreciative Inquiry

No. 2 - Assertiveness and Self Control

No. 3 - Attention Management

No. 4 - Body Language Basics

No. 5 - Business Acumen

No. 6 - Business and Etiquette

No. 7 - Change Management

No. 8 - Coaching and Mentoring

No. 9 - Communications Strategies

No. 10 - Conflict Resolution

No. 11 - Creative Problem Solving

No. 12 - Delivering Constructive Criticism

No. 13 - Developing Creativity

No. 14 - Developing Emotional Intelligence

No. 15 - Developing Interpersonal Skills

No. 16 - Developing Social Intelligence

No. 17 - Employee Motivation

No. 18 - Facilitation Skills

No. 19 - Goal Setting and Getting Things Done

No. 20 - Knowledge Management Fundamentals

No. 21 - Leadership and Influence

No. 22 - Lean Process and Six Sigma Basics

No. 23 - Managing Anger

No. 24 - Meeting Management

No. 25 - Negotiation Skills

No. 26 - Networking Inside a Company

No. 27 - Networking Outside a Company

No. 28 - Office Politics for Managers

No. 29 - Organizational Skills

No. 30 - Performance Management

No. 31 - Presentation Skills

No. 32 - Public Speaking

No. 33 - Servant Leadership

www.ingramcontent.com/pod-product-compliance
Lightning Source LLC
Chambersburg PA
CBHW060705280326
41933CB00012B/2306